21st Century Junior Library

Ichthyosaur

by Josh Gregory

CHERRY LAKE PUBLISHING * ANN ARBOR, MICHIGAN

Published in the United States of America by Cherry Lake Publishing
Ann Arbor, Michigan
www.cherrylakepublishing.com

Content Adviser: Gregory M. Erickson, PhD, Paleontologist, Department of Biological
Science, Florida State University, Tallahassee, Florida

Reading Adviser: Marla Conn, ReadAbility, Inc.

Photo Credits: Cover background, ©Maik Schrödter/Dreamstime.com; cover foreground and page 8,
©Universal Images Group Limited/Alamy; page 4, ©Stocktrek Images, Inc./Alamy; page 6,
©Florilegius/Alamy; page 10, ©Art Directors & TRIP/Alamy; page 12, ©Sabena Jane Blackbird/
Alamy; page 14, ©Russell Shively/Alamy; pages 16, and 18, ©Michael Rosskothen/Shutterstock, Inc.;
page 20, ©Jack Sullivan/Alamy.

LIBRARY OF CONGRESS CATALOGING-IN-PUBLICATION DATA
Gregory, Josh.
  Ichthyosaur/by Josh Gregory.
    p. cm.—(21st century junior library. Dinosaurs and prehistoric animals)
  Summary: "Learn all about the life of the Ichthyosaur"—Provided by publisher.
  Audience: K to grade 3.
  Includes bibliographical references and index.
  ISBN 978-1-62431-166-6 (lib. bdg.)—ISBN 978-1-62431-232-8 (e-book)—
ISBN 978-1-62431-298-4 (pbk.)
  1. Ichthyosaurus—Juvenile literature. 2. Marine reptiles, Fossil—Juvenile literature. I. Title.
  QE862.I2G74 2014
  567.9'37—dc23   2013004922

Cherry Lake Publishing would like to acknowledge the work of
The Partnership for 21st Century Skills.
Please visit www.p21.org for more information.

Printed in the United States of America
Corporate Graphics Inc.
July 2013
CLFA13

CONTENTS

Ichthyosaurs were among the many prehistoric underwater animals.

What Was an Ichthyosaur?

When you think about **prehistoric** animals, you probably think of dinosaurs. But dinosaurs were not the only animals living millions of years ago. Ichthyosaurs were another type of prehistoric animal. These ocean **reptiles** lived between 250 and 90 million years ago.

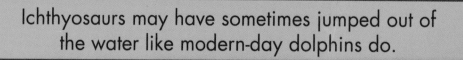

Ichthyosaurs may have sometimes jumped out of
the water like modern-day dolphins do.

The name *ichthyosaur* means "fish lizard." But ichthyosaurs were not fish. They were not dinosaurs either. They are related to lizards and snakes that live today.

Like dinosaurs, ichthyosaurs are **extinct**. None of them are living today.

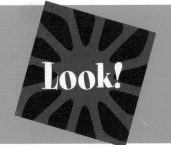

Look! Look at a picture of an ichthyosaur. Now look at some fish and lizards. How are ichthyosaurs like fish or lizards? How are they different?

Can you point to this ichthyosaur's tail and dorsal fin? How many fins do you count on one side?

What Did an Ichthyosaur Look Like?

Ichthyosaurs looked a lot like porpoises and dolphins. They had long bodies with tails. They also had fins and long, pointy noses. Each ichthyosaur had four fins. Two fins were located on each side of its body. Some types of ichthyosaur also had a single **dorsal fin** on their backs.

This artwork in Berlin-Ichthyosaur State Park in Nevada shows how big some ichthyosaurs could be.

Some ichthyosaurs were about the size of a modern dolphin. They were around 7 to 10 feet (2 to 3 meters) long. Others were much longer. The longest one discovered so far was more than 70 feet (21 m) long. That is about three-fourths the length of a professional basketball court!

Eye socket

Scientists estimate the size of an ichthyosaur's eyes by looking at its eye sockets. Large eye sockets mean the animal had large eyes.

Some ichthyosaurs had very large eyes. Scientists learned this by looking at ichthyosaur **skulls**. One type of ichthyosaur had eyes the size of soccer balls! Scientists believe that this ichthyosaur probably lived in deep water. It is very dark in the deep parts of the ocean. Big eyes helped the ichthyosaur see.

Think!

Why is it so dark deep in the ocean? Think about where light comes from. What might stop it from reaching deep below the water's surface?

Mouth

An Ichthyosaur's long mouth was filled with teeth.

Ichthyosaurs had long, narrow mouths full of teeth. Different types of ichthyosaurs had different types of mouths and teeth. One type of ichthyosaur had a short lower jaw. Its upper jaw was long. The teeth on its upper jaw stuck out sideways!

Ichthyosaurs were master swimmers.

How Did an Ichthyosaur Live?

Ichthyosaurs lived in water. As a result, they spent a lot of time swimming. Their tails flipped back and forth. This pushed the ichthyosaur forward. The fins on their sides helped them change direction. Fins also helped ichthyosaurs slow down.

Ichthyosaurs hunted other animals for food.

Ichthyosaurs were **predators**. They chased after other sea creatures for food. Ichthyosaurs used their long mouths to bite down. Ichthyosaurs ate mostly ancient sea animals similar to today's squids. Sometimes they also ate fish and other ocean animals.

Experts are careful not to damage fossils when they study them or put them on display.

Ichthyosaurs needed to breathe air even though they lived in water. This means they had to come up to the surface to breathe. They probably didn't ever leave the water completely, though.

If you want to see an ichthyosaur, visit a museum. They might have some **fossils** to look at!

Make a Guess!

Scientists study ichthyosaurs by looking at fossils. What kinds of things can fossils tell us about an animal? What kinds of things are harder to learn from fossils?

GLOSSARY

dorsal fin (DOR-suhl FIN) a fin located on an animal's back

extinct (ik-STINGKT) describing a type of plant or animal that has completely died out

fossils (FAH-suhlz) the preserved remains of living things from thousands or millions of years ago

predators (PRED-uh-turz) animals that live by hunting other animals for food

prehistoric (pree-his-TOR-ik) belonging to a time before history was recorded in written form

reptiles (REP-tilez) cold-blooded animals that have backbones and usually reproduce by laying eggs

skulls (SKUHLZ) the bones that make up an animal's head

FIND OUT MORE

BOOKS

Dahl, Michael. *Monster Fish: The Adventure of the Ichthyosaurs.* Minneapolis: Picture Window Books, 2005.

Korb, Rena. *Discovering Ichthyosaurus.* Edina, MN: Magic Wagon, 2008.

WEB SITES

BBC Nature—Ichthyosaurs
www.bbc.co.uk/nature/life /Ichthyosaur#p00bndqh
Watch a video that shows ichthyosaur fossils.

Ichthyosaur Page
www.ucmp.berkeley.edu/people /motani/ichthyo/index.html
Read more about ichthyosaurs.

INDEX

ABOUT THE AUTHOR

Josh Gregory writes and edits books for kids. He lives in Chicago, Illinois.